Contents

A world of plants — 4

Seeds and shoots — 6

Roots — 8

Roots and shoots—by numbers! — 10

Leaves — 12

Photosynthesis — 14

Leaves—by numbers! — 16

Flowers — 18

Fruit — 20

Plant reproduction—by numbers! — 22

Stems — 24

Transportation — 26

Working together — 28

Glossary — 30
Find out more — 31
Index — 32

Some words are shown in bold, **like this**. You can find out what they mean by looking in the glossary.

A world of plants

From space, our planet looks like a blue and green ball. The blue is the oceans, and the green colour is caused by the plants that cover huge areas of land. There are even plants living in the oceans!

The number of different plants on Earth is truly amazing. From tiny one-celled algae to the tallest trees, plants can live in all sorts of different habitats. Some are **adapted** to live in deserts, where there is very little water. Others can live in cold, windy tundra regions.

Although plants can be very different, most of them have similar structures. Many well-known plants make flowers and seeds. They have stems, roots and leaves, and they are able to transport water and **nutrients** throughout their structures. But there are many other types of plants, such as mosses. They have different structures and life cycles.

EARTH BY NUMBERS

The smallest known flowering plant is a type of duckweed called watermeal. These tiny plants are each about the size of a cake sprinkle. In contrast, the world's tallest tree is about as high as a 40-storey building!

Plant Structures

Nancy Dickmann

raintree
a Capstone company — publishers for children

Raintree is an imprint of Capstone Global Library Limited, a company incorporated in England and Wales having its registered office at 264 Banbury Road, Oxford, OX2 7DY – Registered company number: 6695582

www.raintree.co.uk
myorders@raintree.co.uk

Text © Capstone Global Library Limited 2019
The moral rights of the proprietor have been asserted.

Produced for Raintree by Calcium
Editors: Sarah Eason and Harriet McGregor
Designer: Paul Myerscough
Originated by Capstone Global Library Limited © 2018
Printed and bound in India

ISBN 978 1 4747 6536 7 (hardback)
22 21 20 19 18
10 9 8 7 6 5 4 3 2 1

ISBN 978 1 4747 6542 8 (paperback)
23 22 21 20 19
10 9 8 7 6 5 4 3 2 1

British Library Cataloguing in Publication Data
A full catalogue record for this book is available from the British Library.

Acknowledgements
Picture credits: Cover: Shutterstock: Amenic181; Insides: Shutterstock: 5 Second Studio 21, Aaltair 20–21, Adistock 16, Jeff Baumgart 26–27, Dariush M 16–17, Angel DiBilio 29, Fotokostic 1, 24–25, Zack Frank 9, Christopher Gardiner 25, Jubal Harshaw 26, Maxim Ibragimov 6–7, Kan_khampanya 5, Dudarev Mikhail 12–13, Boris Mrdja 12, Quick Shot 4–5, Pres Panayotov 18–19, Siambizkit 8–9, Snapgalleria 14–15, Wang Song 28–29, Craig Sterken 22–23b, Praiwun Thungsarn 10, Bogdan Wankowicz 7, Welcomia 11, Pan Xunbin 15, Yogo 19; Wikimedia Commons: 22–23t.

Every effort has been made to contact copyright holders of material reproduced in this book. Any omissions will be rectified in subsequent printings if notice is given to the publisher.

All the internet addresses (URLs) given in this book were valid at the time of going to press. However, due to the dynamic nature of the internet, some addresses may have changed, or sites may have changed or ceased to exist since publication. While the author and publisher regret any inconvenience this may cause readers, no responsibility for any such changes can be accepted by either the author or the publisher.

These lupines are a typical example of a flowering plant. They have roots, a stem and leaves, and they produce flowers and seeds in order to **reproduce**.

A plant can live on its own, but usually they are found in groups of thousands or millions of separate **organisms**, as in this forest.

Seeds and shoots

Many plants start life as a seed. The seed is produced by a mature plant, and it will sprout into a new plant of the same type. Most seeds have a tough outer covering that protects them, as well as a store of food for the young plant to use. Most importantly, they have something called an **embryo**, which will grow into a new plant.

A seed can stay **dormant** for a long time before it **germinates** (starts to grow). Germination only happens when the conditions are right. A seed needs water, **oxygen** and warmth to germinate.

When a seed **absorbs** water, the parts inside it start to swell. This causes the outer covering to split. The first root starts growing downwards, into the soil. A shoot grows upwards, and the first one or two leaves unfold. The young plant produces more roots and leaves, and it grows quickly.

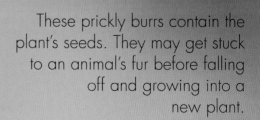

These prickly burrs contain the plant's seeds. They may get stuck to an animal's fur before falling off and growing into a new plant.

For many plants, the shape of the seed depends on how it will travel to the place where it takes root. For example, a maple tree's seeds are blown by the wind, and they are shaped like wings. Some types of seeds can float. Others have tiny hooks that cling to an animal's fur.

The roots' job is to take in water and other nutrients that the plant needs. The leaves absorb sunlight and make food for the plant.

Roots

Roots are the first part of a plant to sprout from the seed, and they are very important. Without roots, a plant could not take in moisture and nutrients from the ground. Roots also anchor a plant in the ground and stop it blowing or washing away.

Different plants have different types of roots. In some plants, including trees, the first root grows straight down. Smaller roots soon grow out sideways. The root system looks like an upside-down version of a tree trunk, with smaller branches coming out from it. Other types of plants, such as grasses, have a thick clump of roots that are all about the same size. These plants do not have a main root.

In some plants, roots are able to store food for the plant, and they often become big and swollen. We eat many of these roots, including carrots, radishes, parsnips and turnips.

EARTH BY NUMBERS

Some plants do not send roots down into the ground. Instead, they are able to get the water and minerals they need from the air, and from **debris** that collects on the plants that support them. These types of plants are called epiphytes or "air plants".

You can often see epiphytes, such as this Spanish moss, on tree branches. The tree provides physical support for the epiphyte.

Sometimes part of a tree's root system is visible above the ground.

ROOTS AND SHOOTS—BY NUMBERS!

A single watermeal plant weighs about

0.00014

grams (1/190,000 of an ounce)
(0.00014 g). This is roughly equal to
two grains of salt! It would take
5,000 of these plants just to
fill a thimble.

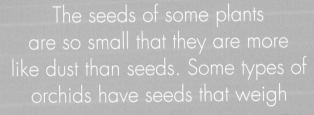

The seeds of some plants
are so small that they are more
like dust than seeds. Some types of
orchids have seeds that weigh

0.00000079

grams (1/35,000,000 of an ounce).
They are 0.0083 centimetres
(1/300 of an inch) long – far too
small to see without
a microscope.

Roots can be huge. The longest carrot ever grown was 5.83 metres (19 feet 1.96 inches) long. The heaviest carrot on record weighed

9 kilograms (20 pounds). But that's a lightweight compared to the world's heaviest beetroot, at 23.4 kilograms (51 pounds 9.4 ounces), and the world's heaviest rutabaga, at 38.8 kilograms (85 pounds 8 ounces).

In some plants, pressure builds up inside the seedpod until it explodes, sending seeds in all directions. The sandbox tree can shoot seeds more than

45 metres (150 feet).

There is a grove of aspen trees in Utah that share the same massive root system, making it a single organism. The grove covers

43 hectares (106 acres), with more than 40,000 separate trunks. Scientists think the aspens weigh 5.9 million kilograms (13 million pounds) in total.

Leaves

Leaves are one of a plant's most important parts. They grow out from the stem and branches, and their main job is to make food for the plant. They also allow the plant to take in and release gases such as water vapour.

Leaves come in many shapes and sizes, but most have a broad, flat part called a blade. A stalk (also called a petiole) attaches the blade to the plant's stem. Some leaves are simple, with only one blade. Others are more complicated, with several blades attached to a single stalk. Some leaves are smooth and waxy, and others are hairy. Some leaves are even prickly!

Most leaves are green, and they get their colour from a substance called **chlorophyll**. In some trees, the leaves lose their chlorophyll in autumn. Eventually, they turn brown and dry, and fall off. New leaves grow in the spring. Some types of trees, however, keep their leaves all year long.

The needles on a pine tree let heavy snow slide off the tree, so that it does not become weighed down.

When a leaf loses its chlorophyll, its red, orange and yellow pigments become visible. This creates beautiful autumn colours.

BY NUMBERS

Not all leaves are broad and flat. The long, thin needles on pine trees are a special type of leaf.

They are adapted to survive in harsher, colder conditions than broad leaves, and they do not fall off in winter.

Photosynthesis

Leaves help a plant make its own food, in a process called **photosynthesis**. In photosynthesis, a plant uses the **energy** in sunlight to turn water and **carbon dioxide** into chemicals called **carbohydrates**. These carbohydrates store energy in a form that a plant's **cells** can use to grow.

Most leaves are broad and flat, which allows them to take in as much sunlight as possible. They also have a lot of tiny holes, called **stomata**, on their undersides. Gases can pass through these holes, and this is how the plant takes in carbon dioxide from the air. The plant's roots take in water, and the chlorophyll in the leaves helps to absorb sunlight.

Once all the ingredients are in place, a **chemical reaction** takes place inside a plant's leaves. Each cell contains structures called **chloroplasts**, where the plant's chlorophyll is found. The chemical reaction takes place in the chloroplasts.

This diagram shows how photosynthesis works.

EARTH BY NUMBERS

All life on Earth depends on photosynthesis. Without it, plants could not survive, and, with no plants to eat, animals could not survive either.

In photosynthesis, plants also take carbon dioxide from the air and replace it with oxygen. All animals need oxygen to breathe.

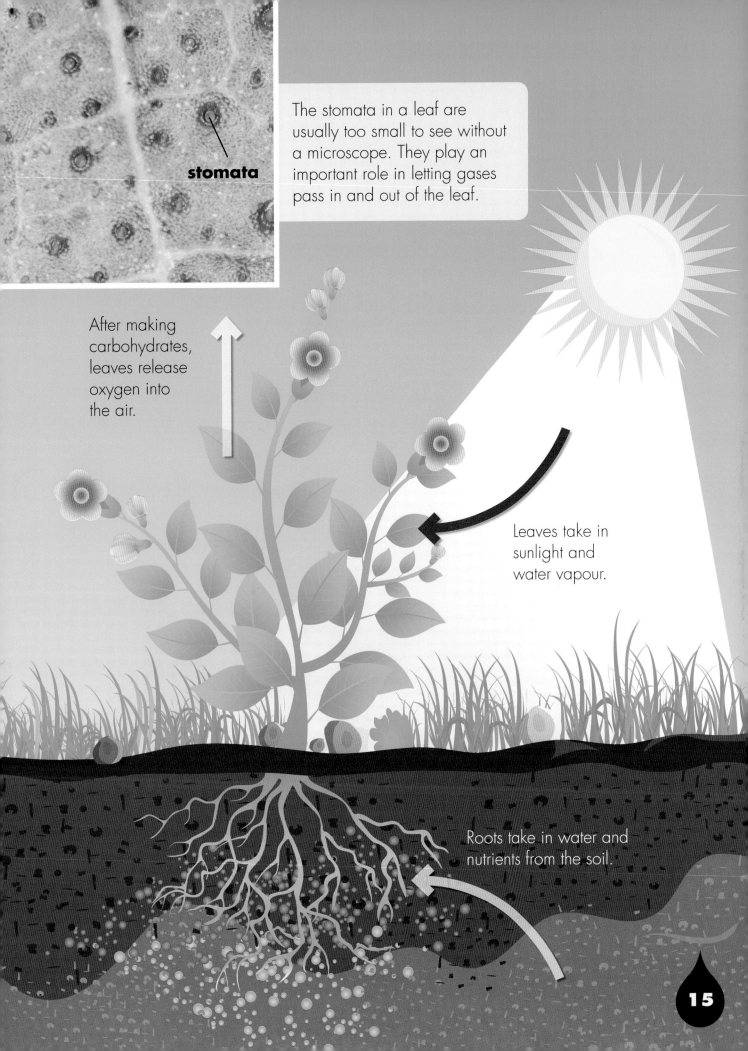

stomata

The stomata in a leaf are usually too small to see without a microscope. They play an important role in letting gases pass in and out of the leaf.

After making carbohydrates, leaves release oxygen into the air.

Leaves take in sunlight and water vapour.

Roots take in water and nutrients from the soil.

LEAVES—BY NUMBERS!

Leaves come in all shapes and sizes, but the leaves of the raffia palm are true record-breakers. They can reach a massive

25 metres

(82 feet) long. The leaves of a wild flower called pygmy weed are much smaller: about 0.12 centimetres (0.047 inches) long.

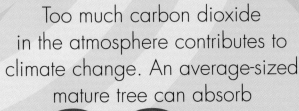

Too much carbon dioxide in the atmosphere contributes to climate change. An average-sized mature tree can absorb

22 kilograms

(48 pounds) of carbon dioxide in a year. At the same time, it releases enough oxygen into the atmosphere for two people to breathe.

Most clover plants have three or four leaves. But the record for the most leaves on a clover is

56 leaves!

A large apple tree may have between 50,000 and

100,000

leaves. But other types of trees have many more. An old oak tree can have 700,000 and a mature American elm may have 5 million!

The stomata on a leaf are far too small to see without a powerful microscope. The leaf of an apple tree has around

300

stomata in an area of just 1 square millimetre (0.0015 square inches)!

Flowers

Flowers come in an amazing range of colours and shapes, and they all have an important role. Their job is to produce seeds. Seeds allow the plant to reproduce and pass on **traits** to the next generation.

Most flowers have both male and female parts. The male parts make **pollen**. The female parts make seeds, but to do this they need pollen from another flower. Insects, birds and other animals sometimes help to take pollen from one flower to another.

When they land on a flower, pollen rubs off onto their bodies. When they fly to another flower, some of the pollen rubs off onto the flower's female parts.

Plants need to make themselves attractive to pollinators. They can do this by providing food such as **nectar**. They may also have bright colours and a strong scent to make themselves stand out. Some flowers are shaped in a way that makes it easier for certain types of insects to land on them.

EARTH BY NUMBERS

Not all plants have flowers. Some, such as pine trees, make seeds without flowers. Their seeds are kept safe in woody cones. Other plants, such as ferns and mosses, produce spores instead of seeds. You may be able to see tiny, round spores on the underside of a fern's leaf.

These flowers look very different, but they all have the same basic parts such as petals.

pistil

stamen

pollen

The pistil at the centre of this tulip is the female part. It is surrounded by the stamens (male parts), which are covered in pollen.

Fruit

The female parts of a flower are at the centre. When the flower is pollinated, these parts start to grow into a fruit. Some parts become seeds, and the parts surrounding them become the rest of the fruit. The fruit protects the seeds inside. It also helps to **disperse** the seeds, so that they can sprout into new plants.

Fruit and seeds are incredibly important to humans, because we eat them for energy. Nuts, peas and beans are all seeds. The list of fruit we eat is very long: apples, cucumbers, oranges, bananas, tomatoes, lemons and avocados are just a few. In most of these, you can see the seeds when you cut into the fruit.

Many fruits help to disperse seeds. For example, a coconut that you see in the supermarket is a seed that was once inside a lightweight fruit. The fruit can float, and this allows coconut seeds to travel long distances across the oceans before sprouting.

An orange tree grows from a single seed, but it can produce hundreds of oranges every year. Each one will contain several seeds.

EARTH BY NUMBERS

Many birds and other animals eat fruit. When they do, they also eat the seeds inside the fruit. Their bodies digest the flesh of the fruit, but the seeds inside often come out in their waste. This can happen a long way from where they found the fruit. These seeds may then grow into new plants.

Most fruits have the seeds on the inside, though they can be arranged in different ways. This kiwi fruit has the seeds on the inside.

PLANT REPRODUCTION—BY NUMBERS!

The largest single flower in the world belongs to the *Rafflesia* plant. It can be

1

metre (3 feet) across and weigh up to 7 kilograms (15 pounds). The *Titan arum*'s flower is even bigger, but it is actually a cluster of many tiny flowers. It can grow up to 3.6 metres (12 feet) tall and weigh 77 kilograms (170 pounds).

Some fruits are truly enormous! The world's largest bean pods can be up to

1.5

metres (5 feet) long. The largest pumpkin ever grown weighed 1,054 kilograms (2,323 pounds).

Grains of pollen are extremely tiny; most are only 10-100 microns (0.0004–0.004 inches) in diameter. A human hair is around 50 microns (0.002 inches) wide. Some pollen grains are much narrower than a hair!

Many plants produce flowers every year, but some blooms are much rarer. The kurinji is a bluish-purple flower found in India. It only blooms once every 12 years. The talipot palm grows for up to 80 years before it blooms for the first time. Once the fruit appears, the plant dies.

Fruits such as peaches and avocados contain only 1 seed. Others have many more: most apples have between 2 and 15 seeds, and kiwis, watermelons and pomegranates have several hundred.

Stems

Most plants are held upright by a stem. The tiny shoot that first sprouts from a seed will eventually grow and thicken into a sturdy stem. The stem holds the plant's leaves and flowers up, and it can keep the leaves in a position that receives the most sunlight. Branches and leaves grow out from the stem.

Some plants have flexible green stems, and others have hard, woody stems. Plants with soft stems usually die to the ground each year. For example, a tomato plant will die when the growing season finishes. In spring, you need to plant one of its seeds to grow a new tomato plant. An apple tree, on the other hand, will lose its leaves in autumn, but the woody trunk stays alive. It will sprout new leaves and flowers in spring.

EARTH BY NUMBERS

Some plants' stems do several different jobs. For example, photosynthesis takes place in the stem of a cactus. The stem is also important for storing water. During the rare times when there is rain in a desert, the stem can swell to hold as much water as possible. When the cactus uses this water during dry periods, the stem contracts (shrinks).

The enormous trunk of this giant sequoia tree is actually the plant's stem. It grows a little thicker every year.

The places on a stem where leaves branch out are called nodes. The areas between nodes are called internodes.

Transportation

As well as holding plants up, the stems of many plants have another job. They make it possible for water and nutrients to travel through the plant. They can do this because of two special **tissues** they contain: **xylem** and **phloem**. These parts are a bit like the blood vessels that carry blood around your body.

A plant's roots take in water and **dissolved** nutrients from the soil. These substances travel up the xylem to reach the plant's branches and leaves, like water being sucked up through a straw. The water eventually **evaporates** from the leaves. Meanwhile, the leaves use photosynthesis to produce the plant's food, in the form of sugars. These sugars travel through the phloem to reach the parts of the plant where they are needed – either for growing new tissues, or to be stored to use later.

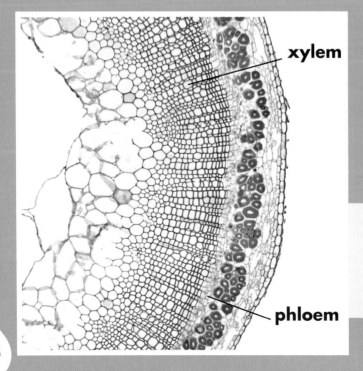

xylem

phloem

The sap from a maple tree is only about 2 per cent sugar. It takes 115–150 litres (30–40 gallons) of sap to make just 4 litres (1 gallon) of maple syrup.

This magnified cross-section of a flax stem shows the xylem and phloem.

EARTH **BY NUMBERS**

The liquids that travel through a plant's xylem and phloem are usually called sap. Maple syrup, which is often served with pancakes, starts as a type of sap. Farmers collect this watery liquid from the trunks of maple trees and boil it so that the water evaporates. After a while, they're left with a sweet syrup.

Working together

Each part of a plant has a job to do. Roots take in moisture and nutrients from the soil, and the xylem in the plant's stem carries the nutrients to the other parts of the plant. Leaves make food for the plant, and the phloem transports the food. Flowers make seeds and fruit to help the plant reproduce. All the parts must work together. It's like the way that your heart, lungs, muscles, bones and other body parts work together to keep you alive.

There are some types of plants, however, that do not have all of these structures. Many plants don't make seeds at all. Some plants, such as pine trees, don't have flowers but still make seeds. Mosses are an example of a plant without a true stem, and the tiny algae that float in the oceans don't have leaves or roots. These plants all have different ways to survive in their habitats.

Each of these sunflowers has different parts working together to help it grow tall and make seeds.

EARTH BY NUMBERS

Sometimes plants must work together with animals to survive. For example, a bee helps to pollinate a plant and gets nectar to eat in return.

The bullhorn acacia plant provides food and shelter for a type of ant, which protects the plant from animals that might want to eat it.

Both the ants and the bullhorn acacia plant benefit from living together. This type of relationship is called mutualism.

Glossary

absorbs takes in

adapted having changed over time in a way that helps an organism to survive and reproduce in its habitat

carbohydrates substances made of carbon, hydrogen and oxygen, which can be used to produce and store energy

carbon dioxide gas breathed out by animals, which plants need in order to make food

cells smallest units of a living thing. Plants and animals are made up of cells.

chemical reaction process in which one or more substances change into new substances

chlorophyll green matter in the leaves and stems of plants that helps them produce food from sunlight

chloroplasts structures in a plant's cells that contain chlorophyll

debris waste

disperse send out

dissolved mixed with a liquid and has become part of the liquid

dormant not active. A seed can stay dormant for many years before germinating.

embryo new plant that is just starting to develop. Plant embryos are found inside seeds.

energy ability to do work

evaporates when a liquid turns into a gas and rises into the air

germinates sprouts from a seed

nectar sweet substance made by plants

nutrients substances that a living thing needs in order to grow and stay healthy

organisms living things such as plants or animals

oxygen gas in the air that humans and animals need to breathe. Plants produce oxygen and release it into the air.

phloem soft tissue in some plants that carries food from the leaves to the rest of the plant

photosynthesis process in which a plant uses sunlight to change water and carbon dioxide into food for itself

pollen sticky powder made by flowers that helps them to form seeds

reproduce have offspring

stomata tiny holes on the underside of a plant's leaf that allow water and gases to move in and out

tissues groups of cells in an animal's or plant's body that are similar to each other and do similar things

traits characteristics that make a living thing different from others of the same type, for example height or leaf shape

xylem soft tissue in some plants that carries water and nutrients from the roots to the rest of the plant

Find out more

Books

Gardening for Beginners, Abigail Wheatley and Emily Bone (Usborne Publishing Ltd, 2015)

Plant Classification (Life Science Stories), Leon Gray (Raintree, 2017)

Plant Reproduction: How Do You Grow a Giant Pumpkin? (Show Me Science), Cath Senker (Raintree, 2015)

Plants (Essential Life Science), Melanie Waldron (Raintree, 2014)

Stems and Trunks (Plant Parts), Melanie Waldron (Raintree, 2015)

Websites

Learn more about the parts of a plant and plant life cycles at:
www.bbc.co.uk/guides/z3wpsbk

Find out everything you need to know about plants at:
www.dkfindout.com/uk/animals-and-nature/plants

Index

absorption 6, 7, 14, 16
algae 4, 28

cactus 24
carbohydrates 14
carbon dioxide 14, 16
cells 4, 14
chemical reactions 14
chlorophyll 12, 14
chloroplasts 14
clover 16
coconuts 20
cones 18

dispersal 20

embryo 6
energy 14, 20
epiphytes 8, 9
evaporation 26

ferns 18
flowers 4, 16, 18, 20, 22,
    23, 24, 28
food 6, 8, 12, 14, 18, 26,
    28
fruit 20–21, 22, 23, 28

germination 6

insects 18, 28

leaves 4, 6, 12–13, 14,
    16–17, 18, 24, 26, 28

moss 4, 18, 28
mutualism 29

nectar 18, 28
nutrients 4, 8, 26, 28

oceans 4, 20, 28
orchids 10
oxygen 6, 14, 16

phloem 26, 27, 28
photosynthesis 14–15,
    24, 26
pine needles 12, 13
pollen 18, 23
pygmy weed 16

raffia palm 16
Rafflesia 22
reproduction 5, 18,
    22–23, 28
roots 4, 6, 7, 8–9, 11, 14,
    26, 28

sap 26
seeds 4, 6–7, 8, 10, 11, 18,
    20, 23, 24, 28
spores 18
stems 4, 12, 24–25, 26, 28
stomata 14, 17

Titan arum 22
traits 18
transportation 4,
    26–27, 28
trees 4, 7, 8, 11, 12, 13,
    16, 17, 18, 24, 25, 26,
    28

watermeal 4, 10

xylem 26, 27, 28